GERD KANTER:
FIVE CHAMPIONSHIP
MOMENTS

GERD KANTER:
FIVE CHAMPIONSHIP
MOMENTS

by Gerd Kanter
with Dan McQuaid

Gerd Kanter near the start of his throwing journey.

Introduction

by Gerd Kanter

As a child, I did not dream of gold medals.

All I wanted was to fly to the moon.

Growing up in Estonia during Soviet times, I was always hearing about the brave exploits of the Russian cosmonauts soaring through the sky in their spaceships. That sounded like a fun job to me, and I couldn't wait to grow up and start visiting other planets.

Later, watching a lot of war movies with my friends, Soviet propaganda films where the Russians always defeated the Nazis, I decided I'd rather be a general. Leading troops to victory on the battlefield seemed even more exciting than exploring the universe.

Then, Michael Jordan and the Chicago Bulls started winning championships, and my friends and I became obsessed with basketball. We'd spend all our free time on the court dribbling and shooting with our tongues sticking out, trying our best to "be like Mike." So that became my new dream. I would be a star in the NBA.

This dream felt more real than the others. Maybe that's why it ended up breaking my heart.

I had success playing against my friends, and the next step was to try for a scholarship to the sports school not far from where I lived.

The tryouts came when I was fifteen years old and entering ninth grade. It turned out that competing for a scholarship was very different from playing at home against my friends. I thought I was pretty good, but living in the countryside I never had a coach to teach me proper basketball skills, so I was behind a lot of the other kids. Also, I hadn't hit my growth spurt yet and was only 1.79m tall when I tried out. Without exceptional height or skills, all I had going for me was my passion, and that wasn't enough to win a scholarship.

The coaches told me to come to a camp later in the summer and they would give me another chance, but I failed that tryout as well.

Looking back, I can understand their decision, and years later I even thanked those coaches. If I stuck with basketball, I might have eventually been part of the Estonian national team, but I certainly never would have made it to the NBA. And focusing on basketball would have kept me from ever getting serious about the discus which means I never would have won an Olympic gold medal. So it all worked out for the best. But at the time I was utterly devastated. The coaches told me I could try out again the following year, but I chose not to. I just couldn't face the possibility of being rejected a third time.

So I gave up my basketball dream and enrolled at a regular high school where I worked hard on my studies and looked forward to attending university. It was at this school that I met my wife Liina, which is another reason I have to be grateful to those coaches for cutting me.

I missed the feeling I used to get from spending hours on a basketball court every day working towards my NBA dream, but I had no more thoughts about becoming a professional athlete.

Then one day during tenth grade we had a district athletics championships for the schools in our area. My father, Jaan, threw the discus a little bit when he was younger, and he encouraged me to try it at the championships. The ring was set up on a parking lot behind the school, and with him coaching me between attempts, I ended up getting third place.

That was a fun day, and afterwards, we started practicing the discus together regularly on a grass field next to our house. At first, it was just a fun activity for us to do together. My father was a carpenter, and I had helped him on many projects. This seemed like just another project, only instead of building a house we'd build my discus technique.

I enjoyed our sessions, improved quickly, and after a year of us working together, my father realized that it was time to find me a more experienced coach.

We contacted a club at the nearby city of Pärnu and asked if they would accept a seventeen-year-old boy who would like to compete in the shot put and discus. They were reluctant at first, because they thought it was probably already too late to make a decent thrower out of me, but eventually they changed their minds and let me give it a try.

The name of the club was Pärnu Altius. The coach there, Ando Palginõmm, was a good man who'd had success with many athletes over the years, and we got along well right away. My father raised me to be a hard worker, and Ando could see that I possessed some natural speed and power. I sometimes competed in the sprints for this club, and once ran 11.2 seconds hand-timed in the 100-meter dash. Not bad for a discus thrower!

Pärnu was fifty kilometers from where I lived, and traveling there to train was not easy. I would first take a bus to school in the morning, attend classes, spend some hours in the library, then take another bus to Pärnu for training. On those days, I would not return home until 8:30 at night. Because of this, most weeks I only trained in Pärnu for two sessions. But they gave me a set of weights to use at home, so I could keep working on my strength, and with Ando's help in nine months I raised my PB with the 1.5 kilo discus by ten meters and won a bronze medal for my age group at a competition called the National Cup.

I've always been grateful for the time I spent with Ando. He was a very good motivator and created a fun, positive atmosphere at the club that made me look forward to my sessions there. I tried to show my gratitude by giving him a trip to the World Championships in 2009, the year he turned 70. Ando loved the sport of athletics and had never been to a major championships before and I was very happy to be able to help him attend his first Worlds.

My time with Ando came to an end when I moved to Tallinn to attend university. As an eighteen-year-old with a PB of 50.40m with the 1.5k, I was still nobody's idea of an exciting discus prospect, but I really enjoyed throwing and wanted to continue training. Unfortunately, nobody in Tallinn wanted to coach me. Everyone thought I had started with the discus too late and did not have much potential anyway. In Estonia we sometimes refer to a clumsy person as a "wooden horse," and I found out later the national coach at the time considered me to be a wooden horse.

Gerd's father, Jaan, helped inspire his passion for the discus.

Young Gerd at home with his mother Imbi.

The throwing ring at the home of Gerd's parents.

Photo courtesy of Raul Rebane

Before he met Vésteinn,
Gerd threw with a lot of passion
and very little technique.

The core of Team Kanter:
Vésteinn Hafsteinsson, Gerd,
and Raul Rebane

Photo courtesy of Hans Ülünke

Photo courtesy of Raul Rebane

Raul Rebane, Gerd, Liina, and Uno Ojand

The only coach who agreed to work with me was a woman named Helgi Parts who coached at the same sports school that had turned me down for basketball four years earlier. Helgi had also gotten a late start in athletics, so she could relate to my situation.

She was born in 1937, when Estonia was a free country, but then the Soviet Union took over in 1940 and right away began deporting to Siberia any Estonian who they thought might cause them trouble. Thousands of people were rounded up and sent away. Many never returned home.

Somehow, Helgi's family survived that first year under the Russians and also the awful times of the Second World War when Estonia became a battleground. But finally in 1949, they were deported to Siberia.

After some extremely difficult years, her family was allowed to return to Estonia, and at the age of twenty-two, Helgi took up sports. Considering what she had been through as a child, and how late she was at starting her career, she did remarkably well, winning the Estonian Championships seventeen times in the discus and thirteen times in the shot put. In 1968, she finished fourth in the discus at the Soviet Championships.

When I met her, in 1997, Helgi had been coaching for a long time, and from her I developed a good understanding of how to train. We did a variety of exercises besides just throwing—interval running, jumps, kettlebell workouts—and I felt like I was improving a lot under her guidance. Like Ando, Helgi was a very positive person and my training sessions with her were fun even though she challenged me with a lot of hard work.

Sadly, I was only able to work with Helgi for a few months because she ended up having a stroke, which forced her to retire. Luckily, she did not lose her ability to speak and was able to return to living a normal life, but her doctor thought active coaching was too stressful, so she had to quit.

Helgi passed away in 2003, and never got to see me become a success with the discus, but I think of her often and owe her much. Without people like Helgi, Ando, and my father, I would have never stayed with the discus long enough to realize my true destiny.

After Helgi retired, I was on my own again with no coach and time running out for me as an athlete.

I was not ready to give up, though, so I continued training mostly by myself with sometimes a little help from one or two of Helgi's former students who were studying to be coaches themselves.

I was also dating Liina, and she was a big help in keeping my spirits up. During the summer, she would often come to training sessions with me to keep me company and to help mark where the discus was landing. During the school year, she would also make us a nice meal every night when I finished training, usually around 9:00 p.m. That was after she had put in her own full day of school and work.

I was studying economics and marketing, and even with Liina's help, the long days of attending classes and training with no coach made me start to wonder if the national coach was right. Maybe I was a wooden horse with no potential.

Then, in the spring of 1998, Aleksander Tammert Sr., the father of the future Olympic bronze medalist Aleksander Tammert Jr., started putting together a group of throwers and invited me to train with him.

Aleksander Tammert Sr. was a very interesting guy to work with. He was a nice person, always making jokes and keeping things lively, but sometimes he'd get distracted by other matters and the throwing group would drop quite low on his list of priorities. This was not an ideal situation, but people were not lining up to be my coach, so I stayed with Aleksander Tammert Sr., and I'm glad I did because he helped me a lot at that phase of my career.

From the fall of 1999 to the spring of 2000, he was able to keep his focus, and I raised my 2k PB from 49 meters to 57 meters, which was very encouraging. In men's discus, 60 meters is the mark you have to hit to show you are a serious thrower. If I could reach it, maybe I would no longer be considered a wooden horse.

But then Aleksander Tammert Sr. got distracted again, and when the summer arrived, I was completely lost with no plan of how to go forward. It looked like I might have a chance to throw for a university in the United States, but I was already close to finishing my degree, which would make me ineligible to accept a scholarship. I was twenty-one years old with no coach, no backing from the federation, and apparently no future in athletics.

Then I met Raul Rebane.

Raul was well known in Estonia as a sports journalist, but I had never met him in person until one day when I was walking down the street in Tallinn and he stopped me. Somehow, he knew my name.

It turns out, he had attended a meet I competed in a few weeks earlier. He was there to watch the decathlete Erki Nool throw the discus, but for some reason, I caught his eye, and now he invited me to sit down at a coffee shop with him.

Right away, Raul started asking me a lot of questions about myself. Was I serious about succeeding as a discus thrower? How could I be when I had no coach and no funding?

Of course he was right, but when Raul questioned my desire, it set off a flame in me and made me realize that I was not ready to give up on the discus. I would keep fighting somehow, no matter what. He saw this in me, saw that I had the passion every great athlete has to have, and so he agreed to help.

The first thing Raul did was to convince his old friend Uno Ojand to start coaching me. Uno had been a shot putter, so he was not an expert discus coach, but it gave my spirits a big lift to have someone there at my training sessions helping and taking an interest in me.

Then, during the fall of 2000, Raul somehow convinced Vésteinn Hafsteinsson to come to Tallinn for a visit. Raul had been in Sydney covering the Olympic Games, and while he was there he asked people from many different countries if they knew of a discus coach who might take me on. He eventually spoke with some journalists from Iceland who told him about Vésteinn.

At that time, Vésteinn was early in his coaching career, so he did not have the reputation he has now of being a super coach. But he had competed in the Olympics and World Championships, and he had trained with some all time greats like Mac Wilkins, John Powell and Wolfgang Schmidt, so I was extremely excited that he would come all the way to Tallinn to take a look at me.

That weekend, Vésteinn put me through some physical tests, and had a lot of discussions with Raul. When it was over, they had a plan. Vésteinn agreed to be my coach. He lived in Sweden, so Uno would continue to be my local coach in Tallinn, but Vésteinn would devise all my workouts and I would travel to Sweden as often as possible for training camps.

This was a huge turning point in my life. If guys like Raul and Vésteinn could believe in me, then I could start dreaming big about the discus. Forget about throwing 60 meters and being just good enough to be considered a "serious" thrower. I would not rest until I had become Olympic champion!

When we started together, Vésteinn warned me it would take many years and much hard work to develop my skills, and he was right. He said it would take five years for my technique to be good enough to compete at an international level, and exactly five years after we started working together, I finished second at the 2005 World Championships.

I did not finally achieve my Olympic dream until 2008. During those years, I experienced many failures, and sometimes, like when I threw 8 meters under my personal best in qualification at the 2004 Games and did not advance to the final, people probably thought I was an idiot for talking about becoming Olympic champion.

But looking back, I am very glad I dreamed a dream so big. If my dream were smaller, let's say throwing 65 meters or becoming Estonian champion, I would have achieved it already in 2004. And then would I have had the inspiration to overcome my Olympic disaster and continue forward? Maybe not.

In this book, I will tell the story of my career by focusing on five major championships. As you will see, my road to success was not always smooth.

Luckily, my gold medal dream was like a tall lighthouse far off in the distance, always helping me to keep on the path, always pulling me forward.

CHAPTER ONE:
2005 World Championships, Helsinki

Photo courtesy of Hans Üürike

The 2005 World Championships in Helsinki were a big turning point in the career of Gerd Kanter.

Gerd's first years with Vésteinn were productive and frustrating. In 2000, Gerd's PB was 57.68m, which ranked him 166th in the world. By comparison, the Hungarian thrower Gábor Máté, who was born the same year as Gerd, was ranked tenth with a throw of 66.54m. Even Vésteinn, who was in the final year of his own throwing career, was ranked 100 spots higher than Gerd.

During the next four years, Gerd raised his PB to 68.50m and his ranking to fifth, but was unable to produce a big throw in the most important competitions. After hitting a solid 63.66m in qualification at the 2002 European Championships in Munich, for example, he managed a best of only 55.14m in the final. Things got even worse at the 2003 World Championships and 2004 Olympic Games, where Gerd was unable to advance out of qualification. Meanwhile, the 2000 Olympic champion Virgilijus Alekna continued to dominate the event, winning the 2003 Worlds and successfully defending his Olympic title in 2004.

The 2005 World Championships, held in Helsinki, promised to be a watershed moment in Gerd's career, where he would either make a huge step forward or confirm people's suspicions that he'd never be the type of thrower who could excel on the big stage.

My first time on an airplane was when I flew to Sweden for a training camp with Vésteinn. I was a little scared when the plane ran into some turbulence, but I was also extremely excited to start this new phase of my career.

My English was already quite good because in high school we had a teacher from the United States named Kimberly. She worked for the Peace Corps and spoke no Estonian, so when we were in her class we had no choice but to speak English to her, and this was a big help in learning the language.

So I could communicate with Vésteinn pretty easily in English when we started together, even though I usually didn't say much during our sessions because I was there to work and not talk.

We would train two sessions per day, and at first it was quite tough because everything was new to me. Vésteinn set about rebuilding my technique piece by piece, and for a while it seemed like there was always a new piece to work on and I wondered when the point would come where he couldn't surprise me anymore. But I was always happy to do whatever he asked.

Our one conflict came when he sent me my first training plan. It was mostly a lot of reps with light weights, maybe fifty percent of a one-rep max. I was on my own in Tallinn when I first started doing this program, and the weights Vésteinn wrote down for me felt too easy. But instead of calling Vésteinn and checking with him about this, I decided to just do heavier amounts. When he found out, he was not happy. Once he calmed down, Vésteinn explained to me that I needed to be patient because we were at the start of a long process and the intensity of the workouts would start low and increase gradually to make sure I stayed healthy.

Our first full season together in 2001 was quite tough. I desperately wanted to reach the 60-meter line in a competition, and I did it many times during warmups, but could not make it happen once the tape measure came out. Even when I started hitting 63 meters in training that summer, I could not reach 60 during a competition. I realize now that I was putting too much pressure on myself, but at the time I thought I needed to throw harder in order to throw farther.

Finally, in spite of myself, I reached 60.47m at a meet in August.

I have noticed over the course of my career that sometimes when you put a lot of hard work into your body during a season, you get the results the following year, and that is what happened in 2002 when I threw over 60 meters in nearly every competition and raised my PB to 66.31m.

At my first major championships, the European Championships in Munich, I made it look easy by throwing past the automatic qualifying line on my first attempt, but things did not go the same way in the final.

It started raining, and the circle became quite slippery. It almost felt like sand was rubbing off from the concrete. I threw only 55.14m on my first attempt, then fouled my second. I finally changed into running shoes for my third throw, but by then I was in bad shape mentally and put my final throw into the net. This was the beginning of a sad series of performances at the world level.

When we started training for the 2003 season, my expectations were way up. Because I hit 66 meters in 2002, I assumed I would be throwing 64 or 65 meters in every training session, and that was not the case. As I mentioned, Uno Ojand coached me in those days when I was not with Vésteinn, and that winter, I was no present to Uno. On our first training camp in January, I was frustrated over not hitting 65 meters, and so I got tighter and tighter and my throws became shorter and shorter. Uno tried to get me to calm down and focus on my technique, but I wouldn't listen and finally he left the session and went back to his room.

I felt bad about this and knew that I should listen to my coach instead of trying to slam every throw, but I was young and stubborn and wanted success immediately, not two or three years in the future.

Some of the pressure was also coming from my dad, who was my biggest supporter but sometimes also my biggest critic. He was not the kind of guy to say "I'm proud of you" very often, so it gave me a very special feeling when he told me how happy he was after I made that 66.31m throw in 2002.

But he also made it clear that I needed to start throwing far in every training session if I was going to compete with the best throwers, and that is what I had in my head at the training camp with Uno in 2003.

Once I started relying on my rhythm instead of going all out on every training throw, I was able to improve a lot and going into the 2003 World Championships in Paris, I had thrown 64 meters or better in ten different competitions. I was hoping to at least finish in the top eight there, but in qualification I threw only 56.63m, the worst mark by everyone except for two guys who fouled every attempt!

Then, in 2004, I threw at least 66 meters in seven competitions leading up to the Olympic Games, including a PB of 68.50m in a stadium in Seville. That made a lot of people think I should take a medal in Athens, but I failed once again in qualification when I threw 60.05m. It took only 61.91m to advance, so this was extremely frustrating.

Besides not wanting to disappoint my father, I also felt pressure to live up to the expectations of the people who had started sponsoring me. When I first met Raul, I had none of the basic things a professional thrower needs for training, not even a decent pair of discus shoes.

Vésteinn told us it would take at least five years for my technique to develop to the point where I could succeed at the international level, and in the meantime, I would need money for food, travel, equipment and other expenses. Luckily, Raul was able to use his media connections to bring attention to my situation and get me connected with sponsors.

My very first sponsor was a local kebab place in Tallinn where I could go anytime and eat for free. By 2004, I had other sponsors as well, which was extremely helpful, but after I failed in Paris and Athens, I started to wonder how much longer they would stick with me.

Lucky for me, my wife Liina was always there supporting me and helping me through the hardest days. She was not able to travel to Athens for the 2004 Olympics because we could not afford it, so she made an audiotape and asked Raul's wife to give it to me after I competed. On the tape, Liina shared her feelings for me and told me that if I had performed well, great, but if I had not, she would still love me no matter what, and had faith that I would succeed in the future. Those were just the words I needed after my humiliation in the qualification round, and with Liina's support and the support of Raul and Vésteinn, I was able to have a strong finish to my 2004 season.

But in 2005, there would be another World Championships, this time in Helsinki, which is close by to Tallinn, so I knew there would be a lot of pressure to take a medal there.

We went on our usual training camp to California that spring, and I got my first 70-meter throw at a meet in Chula Vista. There was a little shadow over this competition because we actually did two competitions in one day. It rained quite a bit before we first started throwing, and so the ring was slick. I was in great shape and still threw 66.24m, but then the conditions improved so much we asked the officials if we could hold a second competition right away.

There was some discussion later about whether or not this was legal, but at the time I was just very happy to have thrown 70 meters, which was a big goal for me.

Another goal was to start winning meets against Virgilijus Alekna.

Virgilijus is a super nice guy, and even though I was trying to knock him off the top spot, he was always friendly to me. If we happened to be together at a training camp we would talk quite a bit. His English was not great, so I practiced my Russian on him, and we managed to communicate pretty well.

At that point, I had only ever beaten him in one competition. That was in France in 2004 when we both threw shitty, but I threw a little less shitty and beat him with 63.81m. Other than that, no matter how well I performed he always beat me, often on his final throw.

This continued in 2005. At the Alekna Invitational in Vilnius on June 9th, I threw 67.47m and Virgilijus beat me with 67.81m. A couple of days later in Tartu, I threw 66.87m and he won with 68.94m. In Lausanne, I threw 68.32m but again finished second when Virgilijus threw 70.53m. It was the same in Rethymno, although he beat me by a wide margin when he hit 70.58m to my 65.57m.

One thing we knew for sure was that if I was ever going to beat Virgilijus at a major championships, I had to start performing better in qualification rounds. Because there are only one or sometimes two major championships per season, it can take years to get comfortable with the unusual demands of qualification. In order to accelerate this process, Vésteinn and I began simulating the conditions of a qualification round regularly in our training sessions.

We'd designate a spot at our training facility and pretend it was the call room like they have at major championships. I would sit there for a long time, just like at a Worlds or Olympics, then take only two "warmup" throws with a ten-minute wait in between, also just like at a Worlds or Olympics. Then I would have three attempts to reach 64.50m, which was around the automatic qualifying distance at most championships. Between each attempt, I would wait for twenty minutes, which is typical during qualification because the flights are so big. The wait between throws can be very difficult. In a normal training session, if you make a bad throw you just step back into the ring and try to fix it. During qualification at a championships, you have to wait while fifteen or eighteen other guys take their turn, and that gives you plenty of time to start thinking about how embarrassing it will be if you fail. This is why even medal contenders sometimes struggle in qualification.

During the summer of 2005, we probably did ten of those practice qualifications, and I failed in at least half of them. But I felt much better prepared when it came time for the World Championships.

Another big change was that after my failure in Athens, we decided to simplify my windup. Vésteinn always admired guys like Mac Wilkins and Wolfgang Schmidt who did a very long, smooth-looking windup at the back of the ring as they began their throw, and so at first I tried to do this also.

But we finally realized that this type of start was not right for me. The long windup made it harder to maintain my balance early on in the throw, and this hurt my consistency, especially in the biggest competitions. It is one thing to show up for a World Championships or Olympic Games in great physical shape, but it is quite another matter to learn to control your power and speed in a high-pressure situation, and my windup was making it hard for me to do this.

So we started using the very simple windup that I became known for later in my career, and this made me feel much more comfortable at the back of the ring. In a way, it was a small fix, but it ended up making a huge difference.

It also helped that in Helsinki we had evening qualification, which always feels more comfortable. If you have a 10:00 a.m. qualification, you have to wake up early to eat and travel to the stadium, which makes you feel more nervous and makes it harder to sleep well. Sometimes, I'd just be looking at the clock the night before an early qualification, watching the hours go by wishing I could fall asleep. That can put you in a very shitty mood.

But in Helsinki I was able to sleep soundly, knowing I could get up at a normal time the next morning and have the day to get myself ready to compete.

Another thing also happened that made me more confident. I threw lousy at the final competition before the Worlds. This meeting was also in Finland, and I threw 66.32m, which is not so bad, but because of my struggles in qualification at major championships, we were focusing a lot on my first three throws, and after three rounds in this pre-competition, my best mark was only 61.30m.

This was a bit alarming, but over the course of my career, I came to realize that a poor outing right before a major championships could be a good thing because it put me in just the right frame of mind going into qualification. If I had perfect rhythm in the pre-competition, then I would probably relax and assume I would have that same feeling when it came time for the qualification round. Then, if my first throw went badly, I would have no plan B, no strategy to get myself back on course.

Gerd with his friend and nemesis Virgilijus Alekna at the 2005 World Championships.

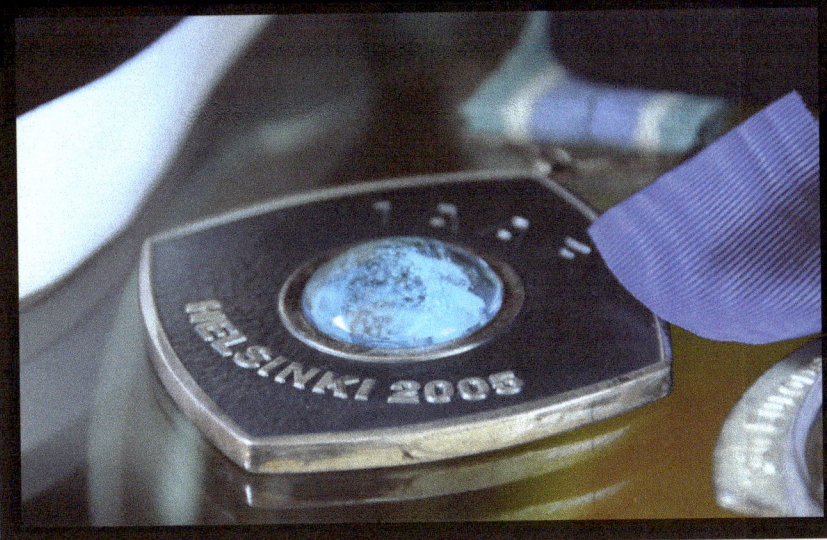

Gerd's first championships medal, the silver he took in Helsinki.

But after a poor competition or training session, we would always make a plan for how to regain my rhythm, and if my first attempts in qualification went poorly, I would just remind myself to stick to the plan.

That's how it worked out in Helsinki.

I began with a mistake when I lined up in the wrong spot at the back of the ring and as a result put my first attempt out of the sector to the left. But I stayed calm, made an easy adjustment, and my second attempt was 65.76m, the best throw in qualification except for one person. Can you guess who? Yes, Virgilijus. He threw 68.79m.

After I made it through to the final, my next goal was to fight for a medal. Virgilijus was in great shape, so it looked like it would be a walk in the park for him but he seemed to be very tense in the early rounds. He got 68.10m on his third throw, but that still left the door open at least a little bit for me.

I started with a foul, but then threw 64.69m and 65.10m which put me in third place behind Virgilijus and Michael Möllenbeck, so I knew I'd at least make the top eight. I hadn't really found a good feel for my throw in the first three rounds, but then on my fourth attempt I experienced something I will never forget. The feeling when I released the discus was so special, it was like some kind of lightning was going through my body. This is something I had never felt before and never felt again after.

That throw was 68.57m, and it put me in the lead.

Virgilijus still had three tries to surpass me, though, so it was by no means a secure feeling. He threw 66.75m on his fourth attempt, and then fouled in round five. I did not improve in rounds five or six, and since they did not reorder for the sixth round in those days, Virgilijus had the final throw of the competition.

I could see right away when the discus left his hand that it was going to be a long throw. I started applauding him as he walked out of the cage, and then the measurement showed I was right. His throw was 70.17m, a Championships record.

But I didn't care. For me, after four years of hard experiences in championships, it was a victory to take a medal, and at that point silver tasted just like gold. Because Tallinn was so close, there were lots of Estonian fans there waving flags, which made the moment even more special. My father was there, and the camera showed him crying afterwards. I think a lot of Estonians shared his sense of relief that I had finally lived up to my potential at a championships. I was relieved as well!

We had this tradition that after a medal ceremony our federation would organize a reception somewhere near the stadium, at a pub maybe where people could gather to celebrate. Fans would come and get pictures and autographs. That year, the president of Estonia attended. Besides my silver, our javelin thrower Andrus Värnik won the gold, so it was a very festive occasion.

Looking back, I can say the reason I finally did well at a major championships was that in 2005 I finally had the confidence I needed to succeed in that environment. Rarely does everything go perfect at a major championships. It is not unusual for even the best throwers to need three attempts to hit the mark in qualification, or to take three or four rounds to find their rhythm in a final. To survive, you have to learn to stay focused and positive in spite of all the pressure, and this takes time.

In Helsinki, I finally felt like there was nothing that could happen which I couldn't handle. Even if the weather turned bad, I knew I was ready. Earlier in the season, thanks to some friends of Raul I was able to visit the stadium in Helsinki and test out the circle. We could tell that there might be trouble with footing if rain came during the World Championships, so we had special shoes made by a shoemaker who removed the soles and hard plate inside a pair of Nikes and attached new soles made of softer rubber which would provide a better grip in a slippery ring.

It ended up raining quite a lot while we were in Helsinki for the Worlds. During our final throwing session, a hard rain flooded the field and we had to take off our shoes and wade through 40 centimeters of water to get back to our bus.

Before, when I was less experienced and less prepared, I might have felt a lot of stress worrying about whether or not it would rain during the competition, but this time I knew I was ready for anything.

So I did not panic when I put my first attempt in qualification out of the sector, or when I fouled my first throw in the final. I stayed calm and kept to the plan. That was the difference between the success I had in Helsinki as compared to my disasters in Paris and Athens.

The season continued after the Worlds, and Virgilijus did not miss one final chance to torment me. A few days later, at the Zurich Golden League meeting, he even "stole" a watch from me. It was raining a lot that night, but I still got off a nice throw of 67.92m.

Of course, Virgilijus came back and threw 68.00m, but I could see that he fouled while trying to keep his balance after he released the disc. No foul was called, though, and once again I finished second to him. This being Switzerland, the winner got a very nice watch, so every once in a while when I see Virgilijus I ask him to give me back my watch.

But all in all, I was super happy with how my season turned out. Looking back, I can say that taking silver in Helsinki was perfect. It didn't feel like a loss at all. It felt like a big accomplishment, and at the same time I still had my main goal of becoming Olympic champion to keep me motivated.

CHAPTER TWO:
2007 World Championships, Osaka

Gerd celebrating in Osaka.

Gerd's remarkable improvement continued in 2006, when he threw 67 meters or better in fourteen different competitions, including a massive near-world-record throw of 73.38m in Helsingborg late in the season. These big throws came in spite of a lingering back problem that he and Vésteinn had to figure out how to manage. Gerd ended up performing quite well at the 2006 European Championships in Gothenburg, Sweden, where he broke 68 meters as he had in Helsinki, but once again Virgilijus Alekna came out on top with a toss of 68.67m to Gerd's 68.03m.

Going into 2007, Gerd's mission was clear. He needed to find a way to finally beat Virgilijus in a major championships. The 2007 Worlds in Osaka would provide him the chance to do it.

My back started bothering me during our early preparation phase for the 2006 season, and it was still a problem when we went to Tel Aviv for a winter throwing cup meeting. I was so stiff that I couldn't bend over to pick up my discus from the ground, and I only threw 62.55m.

Luckily, we found a really good physiotherapist in Finland named Seppo Pehkonen who was able to release the tension in my back, and when we went to Chula Vista for training camp in May I was able to do back squats with at least 200 kilos for the first time all year.

I could still not train in quite the normal way, but I threw 69 meters in the two competitions leading up to the European Championships, so I felt ready going into Gothenburg.

As usual, qualification was not easy. I opened with a foul, then threw 61.49m in round two before finishing with 66.71m. Then, in the final, I started with 61.04m and a foul before hitting 68.03m in round three. That throw came within a few centimeters of hitting the net, so I just barely avoided disaster. Virgilijus opened with 68.67m, and I had used so much energy on my first three attempts that I was not able to regroup and challenge him, so as in Helsinki, he went home with the gold medal while I got silver. Aleksander Tammert Jr. finished third with a best of 66.14m, so Estonia could be proud to have two discus throwers on the medal stand.

Virgilijus beat me again the next week in Tallinn and Zurich, even though I threw quite good marks of 67.86m and 68.41m, so I was still motivated to do better as the season reached its final weeks. I had also thrown 70 meters multiple times in training, so I knew I had something left in me.

In September, Vésteinn put together a small competition in Helsingborg, a place that sometimes has excellent conditions. He couldn't get any of the other top throwers to participate, so it ended up just being me, my training partner at the time Omar El Ghazaly, and one local guy competing that day. As it turned out, the conditions were just right for me. I never got a very good spin on the discus, so my best wind was a little side tailwind, a four o'clock wind, and that's what we had that day. My first warmup throw went five meters farther than I expected, and I ended up having a super series including a new PB of 73.38m. I totally missed my last throw and it still went 65 something. That's the kind of day it was.

A week later I threw 68.47m at the World Athletics Final, but of course Virgilijus threw 68.63m to beat me. So for 2007, my big task was to figure out a way to finally knock him off the pedestal.

One big change we made at the end of the 2006 season was to hire a full time physiotherapist named Indrek Tustit. We stole this idea from Virgilijus. For years, Virgilijus had always traveled with his own physiotherapist, a small guy we called his "mechanic." After the back troubles I went through in 2006, we knew it was time for me to get my own mechanic.

So we hired Indrek, and he started coming to my throwing sessions. We began each session with a routine of dynamic gymnastics, and Indrek was always there to help me stretch and keep my back loose throughout the day. We would also do three or four massage sessions per week, and after a while Indrek even started filming my throws and giving me feedback when we were training in Tallinn without Vésteinn, so he was almost like an assistant coach.

Because of Indrek, my preparation for the 2007 season went extremely well. He came with us to Chula Vista for our training camp, and it was no coincidence that I threw 72.02m there.

In June, I threw 70.12m at a meet in Valga, and this was one of my all time favorite throws. That meeting was part of a series of competitions we used to hold in different parts of Estonia to give people outside of Tallinn a chance to see top athletes compete. Lots of spectators showed up for the meeting in Valga, and the atmosphere was great.

The 70.12m throw was my first over 70 meters on Estonian soil, and it was a very happy surprise. It usually took a few weeks for me to recover completely from our camps in Chula Vista. I always had trouble readjusting my body to the normal time schedule, but for some reason I found just the right rhythm and technique on that throw in Valga.

I was feeling really good after that, so it was a big disappointment when I only managed 66.33m a few days later in Olso and lost by four meters to Virgilijus. He beat me again on July 2nd in Athens, and then I threw 70.93m back in Helsingborg at a meet he did not attend.

The next time I went up against Virgilijus was ten days later in Rethymno, Greece, where I threw 68.43m and he threw 69.67m.

A big breakthrough for me came on 25th July on Virgilijus's home turf of Kaunas, Lithuania.

I threw 69.50m early in the competition and held the lead going into the final round. Virgilijus was stuck around 67 meters, but as he got into the ring for his sixth attempt the wind suddenly started blowing. As an experienced thrower, Virgilijus knew how to take advantage, and he put one down the right sector line that traveled 71.56m.

There were something like 7,000 people in the stands that day, and when I stepped into the ring to make my final attempt, it seemed like every one of them was booing me. That got my adrenaline going, and I launched a big one, 70.92m, the highest second place result ever at that time.

I wasn't happy about losing, but I think for Virgilijus it was a sign that I was getting closer and that no matter how far he threw, no lead was safe from me.

After Kaunas, I had two meets in Tallinn which ended a very busy period of six competitions in two weeks. Indrek did a lot of work to keep me healthy during this time, and I felt great when we went to Sweden for a short training camp. I threw 70.16m at a meet in Helsingborg, and then we departed for Japan.

My expectations for the 2007 Worlds were very different from what they had been in 2005. Then, I was desperate to finally show I could compete on the big stage, and winning the silver medal seemed like a huge triumph. Two years later, I felt ready to take my place as the world's best discus thrower. My PB was now 73.38m, and already in the 2007 season I had thrown 70 meters or better at six different competitions. Virgilijus had been on top long enough. It was time for me to knock him off the pedestal.

I was putting a lot of pressure on myself, and one way it showed was that I started to gain weight. We stayed in our pre-camp in Japan for twelve days, and they had a scale in the dining hall where I would weigh myself every day at lunch. Normally, I weighed 128 kilos, for sure never more than 129. During this pre-camp though, I watched my weight slowly climb past 130 kilos to an all time high of 131. The food in the dining hall was good, but looking back I can see that I was overeating as a way of dealing with the stress.

We did a competition in Marugame about one week before qualification, and as usual the results were not great. I threw a best of 67.28m, which was two or three meters below what I expected based on how well our training was going. But, as I said, a little disappointment right before a major championships can be just the thing to keep an athlete focused, and I had to hope this would be the case again in Osaka.

It did not look like it during the first rounds of qualification. I struggled just like in the bad old days, and opened with throws of 56.59m and 58.81m.

As usual the problem for me in Osaka came from being in such great shape and not being able to control my power and speed during my entrance to the throw. I was very excited and this caused me to go too fast out of the back and to use my upper body too much.

Luckily, just like in Helsinki and Gothenburg where I also struggled in qualification, I was able to stay calm and I hit 67.45m on my third attempt.

In the final, I opened with 64.89m, which made me the leader after one round and so probably guaranteed me a spot in the top eight. Robert Harting was right behind me with 64.62m, and then Rutger Smith with 64.32m.

In round two, I improved to 65.37m, but Robert (65.59m) and Rutger (65.98m) both jumped over me.

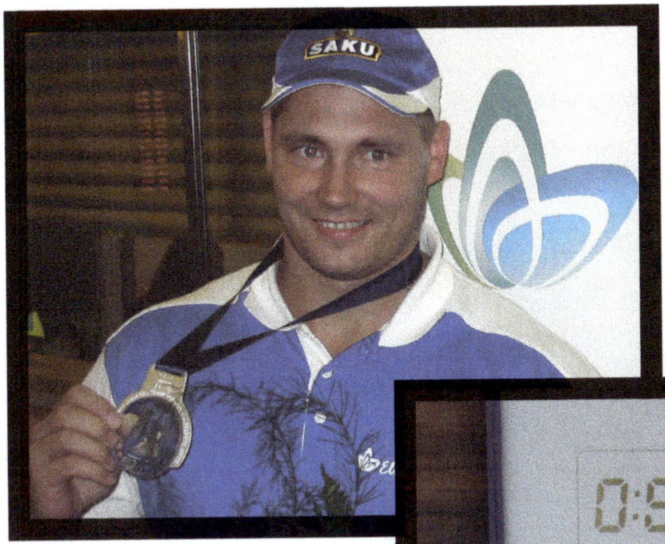

Photo courtesy of Hans Üürike

Gerd shows off his silver medal from the 2006 European Championships in Gothenburg.

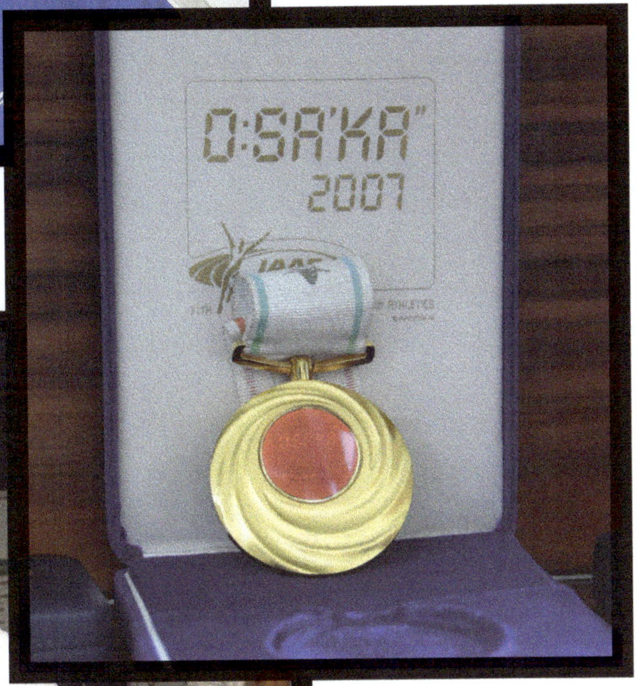

Photo courtesy of Hans Üürike

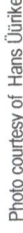

The first gold medal of Gerd's career.

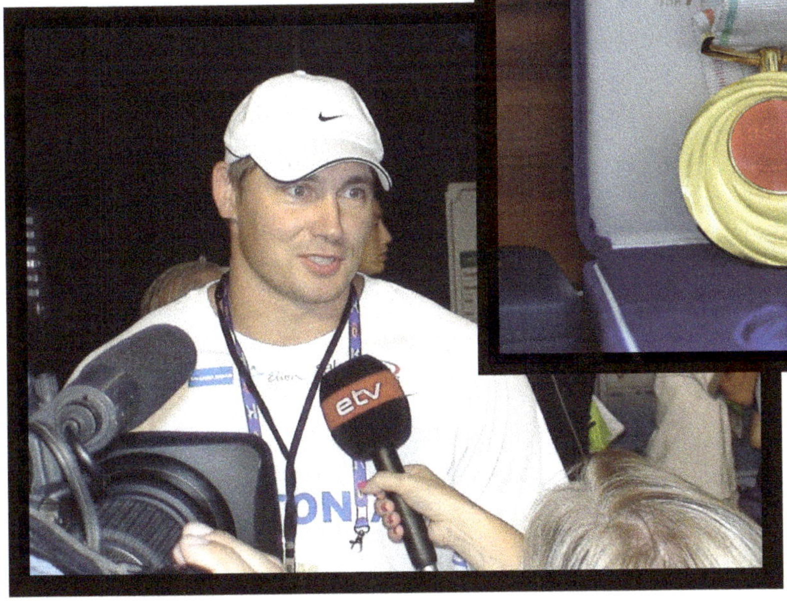

Photo courtesy of Hans Üürike

Gerd speaking to the media in Osaka.

Robert threw exactly the same mark in round three, but I found my rhythm and responded with 68.94m. I cannot say I was surprised by this. At major championships, I always liked to take a couple of throws at the warmup facility before they transported us into the stadium, and that day in Osaka I threw around 71 meters there. So I was in fantastic shape, and I was now mentally strong enough to perform consistently on the big stage.

It also helped that Omar was in the final with me, which gave me someone comfortable to chat with between throws, and helped everything to feel more normal like a regular day at the office. Omar threw very well that night and ended up placing sixth, so I guess we each helped the other to relax!

Rutger improved to 66.42m on his third attempt, and stayed in second place until Robert reached 66.68m in round five. I felt good about my chances against those guys because it would have taken a PB for one of them to catch me, but I also knew I could not relax as long as Virgilijus was still throwing. Surprisingly, Virgilijus struggled for the whole competition and finished outside of the medals with a best throw of 65.24m. I heard later that he got a calf injury during his pre-camp for Osaka, and it made me wonder if he was pushing it too hard while preparing for these Worlds after I had almost come back on him in the Kaunas meeting.

Robert ended up taking the silver medal and was so happy that he ripped his shirt to shreds. Unfortunately, that would not be the last time I witnessed him doing this. Rutger took the bronze medal, which was amazing as he also took bronze in the shot put, although he did not receive his medal until years later when Andrei Mikhnevich, who originally finished third in Osaka, was banned for doping and had his results negated.

My 68.94m held up for the gold medal and I remember feeling very happy and also disappointed in my performance because I knew I was in shape to throw 70 meters. On my final attempt, I walked into the ring knowing I had won the gold, and I wanted to end the competition with a big number. I asked the crowd to do the rhythmic clap, and they did, but then I totally missed on that throw. The fact that it still went 68.84m told me I had a lot more left in the tank. On that night, I had the power to throw over 70 meters and just could not quite manage it.

Liina was in the stands, and it always felt special to have her at the big competitions. Indrek was there as well, along with Vésteinn and Raul, and as usual the Estonian team held a celebration in a local pub. It was a great feeling to celebrate my first gold medal with my team and with the fans.

It also felt good to finally beat Virgilijus, especially with the next Olympics only one year away. And the gold medal in Osaka helped us get more sponsorships, which was very helpful.

Vésteinn had set up another competition in Helsingborg for two weeks later, that he called the "World Record Challenge." We were hoping for great conditions so maybe I could take another shot at Jürgen's record, and as an added bonus Vésteinn got the Eleiko Barbell Company to donate a full set of weights to the winner. Virgilijus would not be competing, and after the year I'd had I was sure I would be going home with the weight set and maybe the world record as well.

But I've noticed over the years that sometimes when you achieve a goal you've been dreaming of and working hard to reach, your body has a letdown and this happened to me after Osaka. I ended up getting some kind of flu and having a high fever for a few days, and I still felt like garbage when it was time for the World Record Challenge.

The conditions were some of the best I've ever seen, so good that I still managed to throw 68.09m even though I was sick, and I was imagining how good the weight set would look in my home gym when all of a sudden Frantz Kruger threw 69.97m. It was a season's best by three meters and won Frantz the weight set.

I was so mad! Frantz lived in Finland, and I figured there was no way he could get the weights home, so I asked Vésteinn to see if he would sell them to me. But Frantz said no, he would find a way to transport the weights. It turned out he had a relative who owned a trucking business and one day a few weeks later the guy pulled up and collected the weights for Frantz.

I was able to recover in time to win the World Athletics Final a week later.

All in all, 2007 was a great season. I won 22 out of 27 competitions, and finished with a season's average of 68.08m. In 2008, I would finally have a chance to achieve my ultimate dream.

CHAPTER THREE:
2008 Olympic Games, Beijing

Photo courtesy of Hans Üürike

A postcard commemorating Gerd's gold medal performance in Beijing.

Gerd finally climbed to the top of the discus mountain in 2007 when he took gold at the World Championships, but his ultimate dream was to become Olympic champion, which he would have a chance to do in Beijing. In 2007, Gerd reached a level of consistent excellence that made him one of the gold-medal favorites going into 2008, but his archrival Virgilijus Alekna–the two-time defending Olympic champion–remained a dangerous foe. Osaka silver medalist Robert Harting also loomed as a threat, as did up-and-comers Piotr Malachowski and Ehsan Hadadi. And Beijing would be the first major championships where Gerd came in as the man to beat. This added a layer of pressure as he embarked on a challenging and ultimately triumphant season.

The Olympic Games are similar to the World Championships in one way. In order to take the gold medal, you have to beat all the best guys. But outside of that, the Olympics are at a completely different level. First of all, the Olympics is only once every four years, which makes it special and also adds a lot of pressure. If you screw up, you have to wait a long time for another chance, and there is no way of knowing if you will still be healthy and at the top of your game when the next Olympics comes around. Also, the Olympics receives a lot more attention than the World Championships. People who love the sport of athletics get excited for a World Championships, but the Olympics gets noticed by everyone, even people who pay no attention to discus throwing or high jumping in the years between Games. And as an athlete, your experience at an Olympics is much different than at a Worlds. At the World Championships for example, you stay at a hotel as you would during a regular competition on the circuit. But at an Olympics, you stay in the Athlete's Village with people from all the other countries, which is a very unique and special experience. Every day when you wake up and walk out into the Village and see all the different uniforms and hear all the different languages being spoken, you are reminded that you are part of the greatest sporting event in the world.

Because of this, when a young thrower starts dreaming about making it big, they dream of winning an Olympic gold medal. That was my dream, the dream that kept me going through the hard days when I failed at the 2003 Worlds and the 2004 Games and it seemed like I might never beat Virgilijus.

And now, as we began preparing for the 2008 season, I felt close to achieving my dream, and this gave me fresh wind under my wings.

The season began with one of my favorite training camps ever in Chula Vista. I was feeling healthy, and we had a really good training group at that camp including Omar El Ghazaly and Märt Israel. We got along very well with the American throwers Ian Waltz and Jarred Rome who lived and trained at Chula Vista, and we had a lot of fun in the weight room there, cheering for each other anytime someone went for a big lift.

I competed twice while we were in California and threw quite well, reaching 70.38m at a meet in Chula Vista and 71.88m, which was my third best result ever, in Salinas.

Then just like in 2007, I was able to recover from jet lag in time to throw big at our first meets back in Europe. At the Ludvík Daněk meeting in late May, I reached 69.62m, which was a sign that I was in fantastic shape. But in the final round there, a nice wind came out and Virgilijus launched one 71.25m to beat me and we were back to the same old "shit" that had haunted me for years!

I managed to beat Virgilijus a week later in Hengelo, but we both lost to Ehsan Haddadi that day when he threw 68.52m, which made him look like a possible medal contender for Beijing.

Haddadi won again at the ISTAF meeting in Berlin, when he and Virgilijus both threw 69 meters while I finished fourth with 66.57m.

A couple of days later on my home turf in Tallinn, Hadadi beat me again when he threw 69.32m to my 67.82m. The conditions were good that day. Also in this competition, Mykyta Nesterenko threw 65.31m to break the U18 World Record. I felt I should have thrown farther than I did, and after the competition, I was not in a happy place. My preparation for the season had gone well, and I was healthy, but it was not a good feeling to be losing both to my old nemesis Virgilijus and also a new kid on the block like Hadadi, and to have a seventeen-year-old like Nesterenko right on my heels!

Looking back, though, I can say it was probably good for me to have a little struggle at that point in the season. Losing to those guys kept me grounded and motivated, whereas I might have become complacent if I ruled the sector at every meeting.

I consistently put up big numbers in June and July, and after the meeting in Tallinn, my only loss the rest of the summer was at Rethymno, where I threw 68.73m but Virgilijus won with 70.86m.

Before the Olympics, we did a training camp in Japan at the same place we stayed the year before when we were getting ready for Osaka. Staying in a familiar place helped to calm me down a bit which was important because everyone on my team could see I was struggling to deal with the expectations that came with being a gold-medal favorite.

As I said earlier, my only expectation going into the 2005 Worlds was to finally make it through qualification and finish in the top five or six. It felt like a big win when I took the silver, even though I was leading in the final round. Two years later, I went into Osaka as a medal contender, but the pressure was probably much worse for Virgilijus. As the defending World and Olympic champion, anything less than a gold medal was considered a failure for him.

And that is how I felt going into Beijing. I was twenty-nine years old, the defending World Champion, and if I was ever going to win an Olympics it would probably be this one. There were no guarantees I'd be in the same shape four years later. One big injury and everything could change. And the younger guys like Robert, Piotr, and Hadadi were already lining up to try to overtake me. So 2008 was my time, and that made me feel a lot of pressure.

Luckily, I performed poorly again in our final tuneup meet in Marugame. I threw 66.25m, which was two or three meters under what I could have expected based on my training, and that competition helped me to get some frustration out and reminded me to be more patient and technical with my throws and not just rely on speed.

I got another reminder in the first round of qualification when I threw only 59.65m. Of course this made me think of my failure in the 2004 Olympic qualification, but this time I had reason to be confident. My technique was more stable because of the changes we made after the 2004 Olympics. We had done many model trainings over the years to prepare for the qualification process. I had succeeded in qualifying at the 2005 Worlds, the 2006 European Championships, and again at the 2007 Worlds. And I knew statistically that my odds of making at least a 64-meter throw were very good.

This understanding of statistics came from a man named Priit Tänava who Raul started consulting to figure out why I was having so much trouble in qualification rounds early in my career.

Priit analyzed all my performances from 2003 and 2004 and showed us that even though I threw 64 meters or better at a lot of competitions, it was almost always in the later rounds. I rarely reached that distance on any of my first three attempts.

That's a problem when you are in qualification for a major championships and you only have three throws to try to make the final. Even in 2005, I was very inconsistent on my first three attempts, so it was a nice surprise that I was able to advance and take a medal in Helsinki.

But I got a lot better at throwing well in early rounds, and by the time of the qualification round in Beijing, I was reaching at least 64 meters on 70 percent of my throws in rounds one, two and three.

This knowledge helped me to relax and to know that I did not have to do anything special to make it through qualification. Even though my first attempt was not so good, the statistics told me that my chances of making a qualifying throw were still excellent.

I proved the statistics right on my second attempt. The automatic qualifying mark was 64.50m, and I reached 64.66m to secure my place in the final.

History and statistics were also on my side going into the final. Raul and Priit analyzed the situation carefully, and their calculations told them I had a great chance to win.

Of course, Virgilijus was still a strong opponent. As I mentioned, he threw 71.25m to beat me earlier in the season. But he would be the first to tell you that throwing 71.25m at the Ludvík Daněk meeting and throwing it in the Olympic final are two very different matters. Also, Virgilijus turned thirty-six years old before the season started, and the oldest discus thrower to win an Olympics was Ludvík Daněk himself. He won in 1972 when he was thirty-five. So to win, Virgilijus would have to make history.

Among the young guys, it was not likely that Ehsan would contend for gold. After his great start to the season, he pulled a pectoral muscle and had not competed since he beat me in Tallinn on June 3rd.

Robert had set a new PB of 68.65m in Kaunas in June, but that was the only time he'd ever been over 68 meters, and statistics showed that it would likely take 68.50m or more to win in Beijing. Also, Robert was only twenty-three years old then, and the only Olympic discus champion that young had been Al Oerter, who won in 1956 when he had just turned twenty. So, like Virgilijus, Robert would be fighting history.

Piotr was twenty-four, also probably too young to win an Olympic discus gold medal, and like Robert he had only thrown 68 meters once in his career—68.65m at a meet in Poland in July. Unlike Robert, though, Piotr had never won a medal at a major championships, and only one discus thrower in history had ever won Olympic gold as his first major medal. Once again, that was Al Oerter in 1956.

According to the analysis of Priit and Raul, there was one athlete most likely to take gold in Beijing.

If you take away Al Oerter, every Olympic discus champion was between twenty-five and thirty-five years old. That spring, I had turned twenty-nine.

Again if you take away Al Oerter, every Olympic discus champion had previously won at least one medal at a major championships. Prior to Beijiing, I had taken World Championships gold and silver, and I also won a silver medal at the 2006 European Championships.

And my season's average going into the Games was around 68.60m, so if I just made an average throw in the final, it would pretty much take a PB from Piotr or Robert to beat me.

With age, experience, and consistency on my side, Raul said later that for me, "avoiding the gold medal" in Beijing was almost impossible.

But I still had to go out and do it.

It was quite warm and humid on the day of the final, but we had the same weather during out pre-camp in Japan, so this did not bother me.

On my first throw, I went 63.44m, while Robert hit 65.58m and Piotr took the lead with 66.45m. I improved to 66.38m in round two, which made me comfortable that I had secured a spot in the top eight. After that, I was focused on winning.

Piotr made it a little bit tougher when he increased his lead by throwing 67.82m on his second attempt, but I still only needed an "average" throw to move ahead of him.

Photo courtesy of Hans Üürike

With his Olympic dream so close, Gerd trained with great passion in 2008.

Gerd celebrating a big throw in California.

Photo courtesy of Hans Üürike

Photo courtesy of Hans Üürike

Gerd feeling frustrated after a poor outing at the ISTAF meeting in Berlin.

Olympic champion!

Celebrating Olympic gold in the Tallinn town square.

Even when I threw badly in round three and Robert improved to 67.09m, I was able to stay calm.

Virgilijus was up right before me in round four, and he jumped into the mix by reaching 67.79m to knock me down to fourth place. But that is when I finally made the "average" throw I was looking for. It was 68.82m, the type of throw I had done many times all season and fortunately was able to make again under the pressure of the Olympic final. None of the top guys improved in round five, so as the final round of throws began I was in first with my 68.82m, with Piotr second at 67.82m, Virgilijus third at 67.79m, and Robert Harting fourth with 67.09m. I would have the final attempt of the night, so all I could do was to try to stay loose and calm while those guys took their last shots at me. Of the three, the one I was most worried about was, of course, Virgilijus. I turned away as he stepped into the ring, knowing that the crowd of 90,000 there in the Bird's Nest that night would let me know by their reaction if Virgilijus went big.

Fortunately for me, his throw of 67.18m did not change the standings. Piotr fouled his final attempt, but he kept the silver and I came away with the gold. The bronze medal was the tenth for Virgilijus in a major championships, and it would be the final medal of his long and fantastic career.

And here was my dream come true. Eight years before, when Vésteinn came to Tallinn and agreed to be my coach, I started dreaming of being Olympic champion, and now it had happened.

My final throw was 65.98m, and then it was time to celebrate. I first ran over to the stands to hug Vésteinn, Omar, and Indrek. Liina was there as well, but security would not let her down near the railing, so I started my victory lap while holding the Estonian flag over my head. There were no running events going on the track at that moment, so I had it to myself. Halfway through my lap, I noticed there were blocks still out at the starting line for the 100 meters, so I crouched down and took off on a full sprint, the flag on my shoulders and the crowd cheering. I'll bet they were surprised to see a man my size move like that, and then even more surprised when I finished by striking the Usain Bolt arrow-shooting pose! The Reuters news service named my victory sprint one of the top ten moments of the Olympic Games, but for me the celebration was just starting.

After a big win, all you want to do is get with your friends and family to share the moment with them, but first there are many interviews in the mixed zone, then the visit to doping control. If you are not careful, that visit can take some time, but over the years I developed a strategy to make it quick. The key is to avoid peeing when the competition ends. Even if you have to go quite badly, you must hold it through all the interviews, and maybe even drink some more water while you are talking. Then, it's just "hand me the cup" and a few seconds later—done! My strategy worked perfectly in Beijing, and then the true celebration began.

China is a long way from Estonia, but even thousands of miles away I could feel what my victory meant for my country. These Olympics took place at the same time as our annual independence celebration. We have a very special outdoor concert venue in Tallinn where 100,000 people come together for what is called the "Night Singing Festival," and it was taking place when I won my gold medal. We were able to broadcast an interview directly into the festival, so I got to celebrate with all those people, which was very, very special.

Also, we had the usual party at a local pub with the fans from Estonia who had made the trip, which was another joyful occasion.

I stayed in Beijing for a few more days, seeing the sights and taking interviews. The New York Times took me to a field and asked me to try throwing a bunch of silly objects like a cabbage, a cookie, a can of sardines, and an actual fish. Of all of them, the sardines flew the best. I got to carry the flag once again, this time at the closing ceremonies, and then it was time to go home.

We have a very special tradition in Estonia that when Olympic medalists come home, they are taken straight from the airport to the city square in the old part of Tallinn. Thousands of people gathered there to welcome me home. The mayor and the president made speeches, and one special present I received was Ene Ergma, the leader of the parliament, gave me an Estonian flag that had been flying over the main tower of the old city on the day I won the gold medal.

It seemed like everyone in Tallinn was there having a good time, except for the two guys who had to carry me on their shoulders from the car to the stage. For them, the ceremony was not so fun!

After the Olympics, the pressure was off and I was able to enjoy myself and throw with great confidence. A few days later I produced my furthest training throw ever, 72.80m without much wind, and in the two meetings directly after the Games I threw 69.91m and 70.32m. At the World Athletics final in Stuttgart, I went up against Robert, Piotr, and Virgilijus on a rainy day and won with a throw of 68.38m.

It was a very fun time where my shape and rhythm were so good I didn't have to think about anything in the ring. Just a nice smooth windup and boom! The disc was flying.

And to top off an amazing year, Liina and I got married in October!

We decided to do a private ceremony at Cathedral Cove Beach in New Zealand, and my luck came with us there. Normally, Cathedral Cove can be crowded with tourists, but on that day there was a storm coming in from across the ocean so most people stayed away and we had the place to ourselves. Just two people in love getting married on a beautiful beach with the storm clouds keeping their distance.

CHAPTER FOUR

2009 World Championships, Berlin

Photo courtesy of Hans Üürike

Gerd and Hans Üürike, who became an important member of Team Kanter, outside the Olympic Stadium in Berlin.

Gerd was not finished after achieving his dream of winning an Olympic gold medal. There would be a World Championships in Berlin in 2009, and he intended to defend the title he'd won in Osaka. There was also the matter of Jürgen Schult's discus World Record of 74.08m which had stood since 1986. Gerd had come close in 2006 when he threw 73.38m in Helsingborg, and again in 2007 when he reached 72.02m in Salinas. But he would turn thirty years old in May of 2009, so if he was going to surpass Jürgen's record, it would need to be soon. Gerd and Vésteinn decided to take a shot at the record in California that May, a decision which would have unexpected consequences.

When Liina and I decided to get married, we kept our plans to ourselves so we would not have to deal with journalists and paparazzi. Some people in Estonia were not happy about us sneaking away to get married privately, but when you have a big wedding, there is a lot of pressure on you to make sure everyone has a good time, and Liina and I wanted to have a special moment to ourselves. We didn't even tell my parents, which made them a little upset, but later when we got home some of my sponsors threw a big party to celebrate my gold medal and we used it to celebrate our wedding as well.

Winning in Beijing gave me a lot of energy to go back to training that fall. I was so excited, I felt like I had even more wind under my wings. Our next goal was to break the World Record of 74.08m held by Jürgen Schult, which we would try to do in California in May. Then I would defend my World title in Berlin in August.

When we began training at the end of October, we decided to make some changes in my training plan. After eight years with Vésteinn, I had a lot of reps in my body, so we cut back on volume a little as compared to previous seasons.

With these changes, and with Indrek's help, I stayed healthy all winter and so when we started lifting heavy in March, I came quite close to some of my weight room PBs.

In bench press, I did a set of three at 210 kilos and back squatted 270 kilos for a set of two. I was very happy with these numbers and feeling good when we opened the season with a winter throwing meet in Tenerife, Spain. There, I showed what kind of shape I was in by hitting 69.70m.

A week later we had an Indoor World Record Challenge in the training hall in Växjö, Sweden, where I produced one of my best technical throws ever: 69.51m with no wind. In that competition I had two throws over 69 meters, and two more over 68 meters. And I threw 71 meters in warmups, which was very exciting. Whenever you hear someone talking about their best performance, they say it was "effortless," and my throws that day felt effortless. I was perfectly controlled in my start, and feeling so good physically that I had no need to press hard on the gas pedal while moving through the ring. The result was a series of throws that were rhythmic, balanced, and efficient. It was the best feeling I ever had for throwing the discus.

At that moment, it seemed that everything I'd dreamed about was coming true. I was the defending World and Olympic champion and in shape to set a new World Record. As we departed for our training camp in California, I felt almost invincible. It was a feeling I would never have again.

Looking back on that time, I realize now that Vésteinn and I were about to make a mistake.

During nearly ten years of working together, Vésteinn and I had had only one conflict. This happened, as I explained earlier, just after he agreed to be my coach when he sent me our very first training plan and I thought the weights he prescribed me to use were too light. I added a few kilos on some of the lifts, and when I told him, he was furious. Vésteinn took the job of writing training plans very seriously. He felt like he'd made a mistake with the first thrower he ever coached, a guy from Iceland named Magnús Hallgrímsson, by training him too hard. Magnús never reached his potential as a discus thrower because he got injured, and Vésteinn blamed himself for this. He was determined not to repeat that mistake with me, so he insisted we take the long view and use a "slow is fast" approach. I would build my technique one step at a time and increase my strength gradually in a way that let me stay healthy.

This system made me World and Olympic champion, but now we wanted something more: the World Record. The way I was throwing that spring, it seemed possible. All I had to do was add one percent to my PB of 73.38m, and I'd have it.

But where was that one percent going to come from?

Many factors combine to determine how far you can throw. Rhythm. Balance. Feel. All of those were going great for me that spring. And I was extremely strong as well. As I said, I had already approached PBs in back squat and bench press during March. But what if I could get even stronger? Could that put me over the top and allow me to break the World Record?

We would find out.

When we arrived at Chula Vista, I kept pushing big numbers in the weight room. It was a very fun time for me. The weight room in Chula Vista had a great atmosphere, with throwers from different parts of the world, guys from my group and also the Americans Ian Waltz and Jarred Rome cheering for each other to make big lifts.

I attacked our sessions there with great passion and put up some excellent numbers: 180 kilos in power cleans, 290 kilos in back squats, 300 in deadlift and 241 for a new front squat PB which was fun because it put me one kilo ahead of Vésteinn's all time best.

I also brought passion to the throwing ring. We were not shy about making it known that we were after Jürgen's record, so each of the three competitions I did in California that spring was called a "World Record Challenge." As you can imagine, I put a lot of emotion and energy behind my throws in those meetings.

And I produced some solid distances. First 70.84m at a meeting in Chula Vista on April 28th. Then 69.86m a week later, also in Chula Vista. Finally, 69.47m in La Jolla on May 12th.

But I did not come close to a PB, let alone the World Record.

And this was the first sign of some trouble to come.

The next sign came when the regular circuit began in Rabat on May 23rd. There was not much of a tradition in athletics in that region, and the 30,000 spectators did not seem to be at all interested in the discus. So it was an odd atmosphere, and I also felt a bit slow and sluggish. I ended up winning the competition, but my best throw was only 65.84m.

Just three days later I hit 68.90m at the Ludvík Daněk meeting, then 67.68m and 69.07m at meetings in Estonia. In a normal year, those would be considered excellent results, but after throwing 69.51m indoors and hitting some of my best weight room numbers in the spring, I could not understand why I wasn't throwing farther.

Even though I felt a bit off, I kept going against the best guys and winning. On June 21st, I threw 67.00m in Bergen and won again. A few days later, I closed out the month of June with my best performance of the summer, a throw of 71.64m in Kohila, Estonia, and followed that with 69.16m in Helsingborg, and 68.26m in Tallinn. I made it through the month of July still undefeated, but still not feeling as good as I had in March before we left for Chula Vista.

My last competition before Berlin was the Estonian Championships, where I threw 68.08m. Anyone looking at my season's statistics would probably consider me the big favorite going into the World Championships, but by the time we arrived in Cottbus, Germany, for a pre-Worlds training camp, I felt like the momentum I'd had going into the season had completely ebbed. I was low on energy, and my rhythm was off as well.

It was a bit of a surprise then, when it came time for the qualification round on August 18th and I pulled off a rare "one-and-done" by throwing 66.73m on my first attempt.

The day of the final, we reported to the warmup field outside the stadium. You can only count on receiving two warmup throws once you are inside the competition arena, so in those days I always liked to take a few throws at the outfield. Getting ready for a big final requires you to walk a fine line. You want to save your energy for the competition, but you also have to get comfortable in your head, and different throwers have different ways to do this. Early in my career, I needed those extra throws in the early warmup to build my confidence. This became my regular routine, so I stuck with it even after I became World and Olympic champion.

There was a nice breeze at the warmup field that day, and as I began my routine, it was immediately clear that the disc was flying very well. I took a couple of stand throws, then one or two full throws with no reverse followed by full throws with a reverse. I never worried much about how far these early warmup throws traveled. During my career, I sometimes observed athletes who wanted to reach a certain distance during early warmups and would keep throwing until they reached that mark. The shot putter John Godina would do this. But my focus was just to get my engine ready for the competition, so I didn't pay too much attention to where my discs were landing that day in Berlin.

But Jürgen Schult was there as a coach with the German team, and he noticed my throws looked quite far. Out of curiosity, he went back later and measured them. He said it was easy to find the marks because nobody else had thrown such a distance. According to Jürgen, two of my throws were between 72 and 73 meters.

I'd had a similar experience two years earlier at the World Championships in Osaka where I threw 71 meters in the outfield before the final. As in Berlin, I was not trying to throw a PB on the warmup field in Osaka. In both cases, I followed my usual routine of pressing the gas pedal a little bit more on each attempt until I was close to one hundred percent effort on the final one.

It might seem odd to produce such distances when I was not focused on throwing far, but sometimes the conditions during early warmups were just right. The warmup ring was always in an open field, which meant that occasionally, as in Berlin, there could be a helping wind. And the atmosphere at the outfield was quite relaxed as compared to what you would be facing once inside the stadium. In Berlin, the warmup cage is located in a quiet park maybe a kilometer away. The athletes and their coaches would slowly gather there, with some taking throws while others just stretched or sat around chatting. The atmosphere was similar to a normal training session, except that your adrenaline would be pumping in anticipation of the competition to come. That combination of excitement and relaxation could produce far throws. Later in my career, I learned to manage my emotions a little better, and to save all my energy for the competition. In Osaka and Berlin my challenge was to find the same combination of relaxation and excitement inside the stadium as I'd had on the outfield. It was a feat I managed quite well in 2007, when I threw 68.94m to take the gold medal. Berlin was a different story.

I hit the cage on my first warmup throw inside the stadium that night, and I let that mess up my rhythm. Luckily, even though I was feeling a little rattled, I still threw 65.91m in round one, which pretty much guaranteed me a spot in the top eight.

But then Piotr opened with 68.77m, a PB and a Polish national record. This was a surprise as Piotr had told me he'd injured his finger earlier in the season and didn't think he was ready to throw well. He said the only reason he showed up in Berlin was because of an obligation to his sponsors!

Also in the first round, Robert Harting threw 68.25m and Virgilijus hit 66.36m, so I got the message right away that I was in for a big battle.

Gerd Kanter and
Vésteinn Hafsteinsson
celebrate Gerd's Olympic
triumph in Beijing.

Gerd and Liina at their
wedding in New Zealand.

Gerd after setting the unofficial indoor World Record.

Robert Harting and Gerd at a press conference prior to the 2009 World Championships in Berlin.

Holding a Gerd Kanter model discus.

In round two, I threw 65.65m, again not bad, but I kept feeling that something was missing. I just did not have the snap I was used to having in major championships since my breakthrough in Helsinki in 2005. And I'd lost the sense of easy rhythm I'd had at the warmup ring outside the stadium.

I was able to climb over Virgilijus on my fourth throw, which was 66.88m, but I could not build from there. In round five, I threw 66.24m while Piotr reached another PB, this time 69.15m which made it look like he had a lock on the gold medal. The best I could do in round six was 65.45m, but Virgilijus fouled his final attempt so I stayed in third place. Then Robert produced the throw of his life in front of his home crowd, 69.43m for a new PB and the win, and once again everyone got to see his bare chest.

It was a nice accomplishment to take another medal and to finish ahead of Virgilijus, but I was left feeling empty. When Jürgen messaged me about my warmup throws on the outfield it confirmed that I was ready to throw at least 68 or 69 meters in the competition, so having a best of 66.88m was disappointing. I guess I could say that I used my nitro too early that night.

But I had been feeling sluggish all summer, even though I kept winning, and in hindsight I believe I was paying the price for overtraining. It turned out to be a big price, too, because never again in my career did I feel as fast as I had before we went to Chula Vista that spring.

As usual, we had the after-party with the fans at a local pub. I was not in the mood to celebrate a big disappointment, but I knew I had to fulfill my obligation as a professional. It is a big deal when an athlete from a small country like Estonia wins a medal at a World Championships, and it would have been quite rude of me to avoid meeting with all the people who had traveled to Berlin to support me. So I went, but it was a very different feeling from the celebrations we'd had in previous years.

My next competition after the World Championships was in Tallinn, and my struggles continued. This was the final stop on the Estonian Grand Prix. I had won each of the previous meetings that year, and all I had to do was to take first place in Tallinn to collect the jackpot. Robert competed as well, and I remember he joked with me that he would lose on purpose if I promised to share the jackpot with him. But he ended up winning with a throw of 66.49m, while I finished fourth with 64.95m, my worst performance of the season.

As usual, I threw well at two meetings in Helsingborg (68.97m and 69.99m) but I felt totally lost at the World Athletics Final and finished fifth with a best throw of 65.43m.

It was a strange ending to a strange season. A year before, I had been on top of the world with my Olympic gold and my marriage to Liina. Now, I was feeling like I'd let people down, almost like when I failed to make the final at the 2003 Worlds and 2004 Olympics.

Looking back, I can see that the difficulties I had in 2009 were caused by going a bit too far past my limits that spring. Trying to break the World Record while in the middle of a four or five week period of heavy lifting was too much, and my nervous system broke down.

If I was going to go for the record in California, I should have switched to lower-intensity workouts in the weight room the way we always did in the weeks leading up to a major championships. This would have given me a better chance of finding my best feeling with the discus so that I could have transferred all my power into the implement. Instead, we kept trying to increase my level of power by lifting at a high intensity in several different exercises at once.

Should Vésteinn and I have known we were taking a risk in doing this?

Possibly. But you do not become a great athlete or a great coach by avoiding risk. You achieve greatness by pushing your limits. It would be helpful if there was a device that could tell when an athlete was getting too close to the line, but there isn't. So oftentimes, you don't understand your limits until you go too far.

After winning Olympic gold in 2008, I was not thinking about limits. I was looking ahead to breaking the World Record, defending my World title, and eventually winning another Olympics.

Instead, when the 2009 season came to an end, I had to figure out how to get my career back on the correct path.

CHAPTER FIVE

2012 Olympic Games, London

Photo courtesy of Hans Üürike

Gerd Kanter later in his career as he fought to remain on top of the discus world.

In the years after the 2009 World Championships, Gerd struggled to find his old form.
His main rival now was Robert Harting, who seized the title of Top Dog in the Discus in Berlin and refused to let go. Another rival was Father Time. When an athlete reaches the age of thirty, they often lose some of their youthful speed and explosiveness, and going forward, Gerd would have to rely more on his experience and toughness and less on his physical abilities. He would also have to get back in sync with Vésteinn as they struggled to deal with the disappointment of the 2009 season.

During my years with Vésteinn, we would sit down after each season and do a recap.
What went well? What didn't go well? What should we do differently the next year?

Until 2009, those recaps had been mostly comfortable conversations. I was always getting better every year and we considered the struggles I had at the 2003 Worlds and 2004 Olympics to be part of the process, so we had very few conflicts.

But as defending World and Olympic champion, there was no getting around the fact that my performance in Berlin was a huge disappointment, especially considering the way I was throwing in March when I set the indoor World Record.

To me, it was clear we'd made a mistake while we were in California. Trying to go for the World Record while also lifting heavy was just too much for my body to handle. When I say "lifting heavy," I am talking about two squat sessions per week from mid-March to the end of April, one day of back squats and one of front squats. In back squats, we often used 250 kilos or more, which made it hard for my nervous system to recover. Add in heavy bench presses and heavy cleans, combined with high intensity throwing and it proved to be too much.

Looking back, I would say we'd have been okay in Chula Vista if we had focused more on throwing and only gone heavy on one lift instead of several lifts at the same time.

But talking this through with Vésteinn was not easy. From the first day we started together, I had always been happy just to follow his plan. And why not? He took me from a nobody in the sport to World and Olympic champion. And I loved lifting heavy weights, so he'd probably have gotten an argument from me if we'd have gone lighter in Chula Vista. But I wanted him to acknowledge we'd made a mistake that spring, and that was hard for him to do. As a result, there was for the first time tension between us.

But we carried on and began preparing for the 2010 season, which turned out to be a very difficult one.

I don't think I ever regained the speed and power I'd had in March of 2009, and the first indication of this was my performance at the 2010 indoor meeting in Växjö where I threw 66.95m, two-and-a-half meters less than the year before.

I threw well in Chula Vista (71.45m and 69.83m), but after going undefeated for almost all of 2009, I finished fourth, second, and second again at my first meets on the circuit in 2010.

Later that summer, my streak of taking a medal at every major championships was stopped when I finished fourth at the European Championships in Barcelona. I hit the automatic mark on my first attempt in qualification, but the circle was quite slippery and in the final and I let that bother me. I made my best throw of 66.20m on my sixth attempt, but it was not enough to take a medal. Piotr won, Robert Harting took second, and Robert Fazekas beat me out for the bronze medal with a throw of 66.43m, which was a bitter moment for me considering his history of doping.

The 2011 season was difficult as well. I chose not to attend the usual training camp in San Diego with the rest of our group because I wanted to avoid the struggle of getting reacclimated to the European time zone just as the regular season got going.

Instead, I ended up spending three weeks in Doha before competing in the Doha Diamond League meeting. The average temperature during my time there was above 40 degrees celsius, which is well over 100 degrees fahrenheit. I think the temperature may have gotten as high as 50 degrees celsius, but the outdoor thermometers were made not to reach that high because they used a lot of foreign laborers and by law they had to give them time off if the temperature hit 50.

Somehow we managed, and I opened the outdoor season on my birthday with a throw of 67.49m to take the win.

The rest of the season was a struggle similar to the way things went in 2010. I won the Diamond League meeting in Bislett, but finished fourth in Eugene, third in Paris and fifth in Stockholm.

Robert was throwing consistently high marks that season and was the favorite going into the World Championships in Daegu. Piotr was European champion in 2010, so he was expected to medal as well. Ehsan Hadadi was also considered a contender, as was Virgilijus even though he was by then thirty-nine years old.

I struggled in qualification and did not reach the automatic standard of 65.50m. But 63.50m on my second attempt was enough to put me in ninth place and secure a spot in the final.

That day Vésteinn and I went to a hotel parking garage in the afternoon and did some drills to stabilize my technique. I felt good after that session and thought if I could just hit some positions I might throw 67 meters that night.

Robert opened with 68.49m and Hadadi with 65.29m while I reached only 62.79m on my first attempt. But then I found a nice rhythm and went 66.95m, 66.13m, and 66.90m on my next three throws. Robert improved to 68.97m and Hadadi to 66.08m, but my 66.95m held up for the silver medal, which was a very nice feeling after finishing outside the podium in Barcelona.

Another pleasant part of the 2011 Worlds was that one of my training partners, Märt Israel, was with me in the final just like Omar El Ghazaly had been with me in Osaka in 2007. Märt was having his best year in 2011. He threw a PB of 66.98m in Chula Vista, then won the University Games a week before the Worlds. He was a multi-talented guy who could also throw the shot, javelin and hammer pretty well. In fact, his body was probably best suited to the hammer. He was very strong with huge traps. But like me, Märt was Estonian and in Estonia the discus was the most popular throw so that's the direction he chose. He came into Daegu feeling loose and confident, and threw 64.19m in the qualification then 65.20m in the final to finish fourth, so we almost had two Estonian medalists like at the 2006 European Championships when I got silver and Aleksander Tammert Jr. took bronze.

But I finished 2011 with a season's average of only 65.84m, the lowest since 2004, which was a sign of how much I was struggling.

After a short rest, though, I felt better going into the 2012 season. I was excited by the chance to fight for a second Olympic gold medal in London, and winning silver in Daegu showed me that I had a chance.

Once again, I skipped California and began my season in Doha.

I was very consistent through my first five competitions, with a best result in each between 65.22m and 66.32m.

Besides the Olympics, there was also a European Championships that season, hosted by Helsinki, a place where I had pleasant memories.

Those memories must have inspired me, because I hit a few 70-meter throws in training with a good wind in the days leading up to qualification. Of course, I struggled once qualification began, reaching only 59.08m on my opening throw. I improved a bit in round two with 63.71m but was still well below the automatic qualifying line of 66.00m. Fortunately, my third attempt went 64.85m, which put me in sixth place overall and allowed me to advance.

It rained during the final, but I still opened well with a throw of 65.11m. Robert took over the competition in round four when he reached 68.30m. My best throw of 66.53m came on my fifth attempt and held up for second place. Zoltán Kővágó took the bronze with 66.42m, but later had the medal taken away for doping, so Rutger Smith ended up with a medal in both the shot put and discus just like at the 2007 Worlds.

It was interesting to me that some of the top guys like Piotr and Virgilijus chose not to compete at the Europeans, probably because they didn't want to interrupt their training for the Olympic Games. But I saw the European Championships as good preparation for the Olympics, and with five weeks between them, I knew I had plenty of time to recover and refocus.

I threw 67.27m at Sollentuna one week after Europeans, won the London Diamond League meeting a week after that, and hit 67.36m at another meet in London just prior to the Games, so it seemed like the Europeans had given me some good stimulus!

Also during this time, I won a very important bet with my father. He was the reason I started throwing in the first place, and I loved having him in Helsinki in 2005 when I took silver at the Worlds. But it was hard on him to watch me compete in the biggest competitions. Those moments were very emotional for him, and he did not like showing his emotions. I tried all summer to convince him, as did Raul and Liina, but he refused.

Not long before the Games, I was home for a weekend and my father and I did a training session at the field by our house where I always loved to throw. I hit around 67 meters that day, and then we went together to see a motocross competition in a town nearby. I was on my feet for five hours watching motocross, and I could still feel it in my legs the next day.

But we were scheduled to do another throwing session, and after I warmed up I told my father if I threw 70 meters that day then he would have to promise to come to the Olympics. He agreed, probably thinking there was no way I could hit 70 meters on exhausted legs.

At first, he was right. I took about twenty throws, and did not reach the mark. On one, I came very close, but it turned out to be 69.90m. He wanted to end the contest after that, but I talked him into giving me a few more attempts. I totally missed my next throw, but then a little breeze came up and I hit 71.30m.

And so my father had to come to the Games.

With him and my mother both sitting close to the rail not far from the discus cage, I once again struggled in qualification. My first throw was a foul, and my second was 59.72m. But after fighting all summer to get my father to the Games, there was no way I was going to bomb out of qualification, so I shortened my backswing even more than usual when I set up for my third throw, and I ended up making the furthest distance of all the qualifiers: 66.39m.

In the final, Hadadi hit a big opener of 68.18m, while Robert reached 67.79m and forty-year-old Virgilijus threw 67.38m! I was happy with my opener of 65.07m because I knew it would get me in the top eight, and I improved to 65.79m on my second attempt.

I was not surprised by Ehsan's 68.18m opener. He was a veteran who won the bronze in Daegu, and was very strong mentally in the big competitions. But after my second throw, I felt like I could catch him. I had lined up that throw nicely until the very last second when I scooped it a little bit. The fact that it still went 65.79m told me I was ready to go big.

The 65.79m throw put me into fourth place briefly until Piotr hit 66.92m on his second attempt.

Piotr improved again to 67.19m in round four, but he was still behind Robert, Ehsan, and Virgilijus, with me right behind him in fifth.

This was Robert's first time as an Olympic gold medal favorite, and the pressure might have been bothering him because he looked like he was struggling to find his rhythm.

Signing autographs for the fans.

During the years after his Olympic triumph, Gerd fought hard to stay on top of the discus world.

As his physical skills declined, Gerd relied more on experience and technique.

Photo courtesy of Hans Üürike

Photo courtesy of Hans Üürike

Gerd faced many challenges late in his career.

Photo courtesy of Hans Üürike

With training partner Omar El Ghazaly.

He could not have been happy then when I threw 68.03m in round five and dropped him into third place.

But Robert was a great competitor, and he responded like a champion. On his fifth throw, he hit 68.27m to take over the top spot.

Nobody improved in round six, so the podium was Robert, Ehsan, then me, all three of us within twenty-four centimeters of each other.

I was a little disappointed because I knew I had it in me to throw farther, but on the other hand I had produced a season's best at an Olympic Games, which is not easy to do! Looking back, I like to call this my shiniest bronze medal. It showed me that I could still play the big game, and gave me renewed inspiration to keep my career going for another Olympic cycle.

The 2012 Games showed how much I had matured as a thrower. When I was younger, I'd get excited for the big competitions, but I didn't know how to control that excitement, and I would often use up too much energy on the warmup field outside of the stadium. But In London, I was thirty-three years old with many years of experience, and I had finally learned how to relax and let the adrenaline work for me.

That's how I was able to throw 68.03m in an Olympic final when my season's average was only 65.78m.

I finished the season by winning my second Diamond League title, and then Vésteinn and I sat down for another talk. At that point, I felt totally in sync with him regarding technique, but I wanted to try a different approach in the weight room.

I felt nothing but gratitude towards Vésteinn and considered him to be the best discus coach in the world. Without him, I never would have made it to the top, but now I simply wanted to try something new. So I proposed to Vésteinn that he remain my coach for throwing but let me go my own way in the gym.

This was not easy for him to hear. Vésteinn took great pride in his ability to plan workouts, and he put a tremendous amount of effort into it. To write each four-week cycle he would spend hours and hours going back over our old workouts to make sure he was using the best possible approach. He also believed that it was vital to properly balance throwing and lifting, so it probably did not seem feasible that he could make a plan without being in charge of both.

But I was at a point in my career where if I was going to make changes, I could not delay. The next Olympic cycle would probably be my last. And so, we decided to part ways.

Over the years, Indrek had become not only a physio but also an assistant coach for me. and now I asked him to take over as my coach full time.

Indrek insisted we find someone with more experience to serve as a consultant, and so we contacted Dan Pfaff who had worked with many Olympians in different events, and John Godina the three-time World champion in the shot put.

We spoke with John and Dan about the best way to train for an athlete like me who was getting late in their career and had been following the same plan for a long time. They said there were two ways to overcome the loss of power that naturally happens with age. One was to introduce new kinds of stimulus. When I first started working with Vésteinn as a twenty-one-year-old, the best way was for me to stick to an orderly, disciplined training plan. That's what we did, and the results were pretty good: eight medals at major championships in twelve years!

But by 2012, I was older and had many sets and reps of training in me and John and Dan recommended that we start to surprise my body with a new approach.

The other way to keep improving as I aged was to adopt a "less is more" philosophy. I had always loved spending time in the weight room and the throwing ring, but John and Dan helped convince me that I shouldn't be worried about doing a little less. They warned me not to break down my nervous system too often with heavy training, because that would make it hard for me to find my speed and rhythm when I needed it.

These were concepts that Indrek and I had already been talking about, but it was nice to have confirmation from coaches like Dan Pfaff and John Godina that we were thinking in the right direction.

Indrek had been a little bit worried about taking over responsibility for an Estonian "national treasure" but after these consultations, he felt comfortable and we moved forward to the next and final chapter of my career.

With Liina, Kristjan, and Piotr Malachowski.

Afterward

Together with Indrek, I won three more championships medals before retiring in 2018. During those years, the biggest challenge I faced came not from younger throwers like Robert and Piotr or the latest up-and-comers Andrius Gudžius and Daniel Ståhl. The biggest challenge was keeping my body in one piece.

As careful as we were about trying to keep me healthy, it became hard to avoid injury during this final phase of my career. In 2013, I began the season with trips to Shanghai, the Czech Republic, Eugene, and finally back to Tallinn, and all that flying made my back feel stiff for the rest of the season. At a pre-camp before the World Championships in Moscow, I tried to do some back squats and only managed one set of five with 100 kilos. The female shot putter Yevgeniya Kolodko was training at the same place, and that day she back squatted 190 kilos for a set of three. Yevgeniya must have wondered how I ever got to be Olympic champion on such weak legs!

In March of 2015, I got a hernia in my right leg that made it painful to use my normal throwing technique. We waited until after the season to get it repaired at a special clinic in Germany. They were very good at fixing hernias, and offered me a deal where they would do both my legs for a discounted price, even though my left leg had not yet ruptured. I said, no, just take care of the right one. The doctor promised that once she fixed me I'd have no more trouble down there, and she was correct.

But then, just before the 2017 season, I injured a pec muscle while bench pressing. I was still able to throw, and opened with 65.87m at a meeting in Wiesbaden, but after a couple more attempts I tore the muscle almost completely through. My right pec still has a small hole where the injury was.

But as my body failed, all the knowledge and experience I had gained over the years allowed me to keep fighting for medals. At the 2013 Worlds, the heat in Moscow was oppressive and my back was questionable, so I really needed a one-and-done in qualification. I got it by throwing 65.54m on my first attempt, which allowed me to conserve my energy and not put too much stress on my back. In the final, I only reached 65.19m, but that was good enough for the bronze medal behind Robert and Piotr. And I was proud of my performance. I did not throw a season's best as I had at the London Olympics, but 65.19m was still better than my season's average.

I had to use my wisdom again at the 2014 European Championships in Zurich, where the surface they put down to try to make the track fast for Usain Bolt (he would run there later in the summer at the Diamond League final) turned into an ice rink when it rained before the final. Indrek and I had a great pre-camp the week before, and I went in thinking I was ready to throw 68 meters. But then I stepped out of the ring after my first warmup attempt and had to grab the net to keep from falling flat on my back. This feeling that you could fall down at any time was quite unsettling, and in the old days I might have gotten frustrated and lost my concentration. But I stayed calm and took silver with a best of 64.75m. Robert won with 66.07m.

My final championships medal came two years later at the 2016 European Championships in Amsterdam. They held the qualification round in a park next to the Van Gogh Museum, and as was now my habit, I advanced easily. In fact, I produced a season's best of 65.13m.

The conditions inside the stadium for the final were not so good, with a left tailwind which gave a lot of people trouble. But I was able to produce another season's best, this time 65.27m to take bronze behind Piotr (67.06m) and Philip Milanov (65.71m).

These results showed how all my years on the circuit, all the traveling and competing, the trying and failing had taught me to throw my best when it mattered most.

I had promised Liina to retire after the 2016 Olympics, but my performance in Rio left a bad taste in my mouth. I came very close to having a heat stroke during the final, and finished fifth. That's not how I wanted to go out, so I talked her into two more seasons. The first international championships of my career had been in Munich in 2002, and so I thought making the 2018 Europeans in Berlin my final championships would give my career a nice set of bookends.

I ended up fifth in Berlin, while Gudžius and Daniel Ståhl battled for gold. A couple of weeks later, my career officially ended with a special ceremony and competition held for me in Tallinn. A bunch of the top guys showed up, including Piotr, Daniel, Gudžius, and Robert Urbanek. Robert Harting did not compete, but he came to the ceremony and made a nice speech.

After that, I shocked everybody, including Liina, by becoming a coach.

This is something I never considered until 2018. That year, Indrek and I began helping our fellow Estonian Martin Kupper, who had been fourth at the Rio Olympics. At the same time, throughout the season I had some conversations with Poitr and with Robert Urbanek about their situation and they told me they were looking for a change.

Finally, at the ceremony in Tallinn to mark the end of my throwing career, they made me a formal offer to become their coach and I accepted.

This was not easy for Liina to hear, especially since we now had a child. Our son Kristjan was born in 2014 and I knew it was hard on both him and Liina when I was on the road.

But the passion that drove me to the top of my sport was still with me, and coaching was a way to stay in the arena and keep fighting for medals. Also, I felt like I had accumulated a lot of useful knowledge about discus training and technique, and that I should put this knowledge to use while it was still fresh. So I tried to make a compromise that would allow me to try out the coaching life in a way that would not be too hard on my family.

The contract I made with Piotr and Robert Urbanek was for two years only. I would train them through the 2020 Olympics, and then assess my situation. Also, I asked that they come to Estonia for training camps as often as possible, so I could minimize my time on the road.

It turned out because of Covid that my adventure with Piotr and Robert Urbanek lasted three years, parts of which were quite difficult. In the Polish system, the athletes go on many training camps, and the federation requires them to always have a coach present. As a fresh coach, I was not good at saying no, and even though they came frequently to Estonia, I found myself on the road even more than I had been when I was competing. This was very hard on Liina and Kristjan. Another frustrating part of those years was my inability to help those guys throw to their potential at championships. Both had solid seasons in 2019, and were in great shape going into the World Championships in Doha, but neither made it out of qualification. Robert did not make it to the Olympics when they were finally held in 2021, but Piotr did and once again failed to advance to the final. As you have read, making it through qualification was something that I got much better at towards the end of my career, but somehow I could not transfer that ability to Piotr and Robert.

Nonetheless, I enjoyed coaching them, especially Piotr. By the time I began working with him, Piotr had already been World and European Champion with seven medals total at major championships. This made me wonder if he would be open to any changes I suggested, but it turned out he was. For a coach/athlete relationship to succeed, it has to be a two-way street, where the coach adapts his plan based on feedback from the athlete, and the athlete in turn does his best to follow the plan. That is how it was with Piotr for our entire three years together, and we remain good friends to this day.

Robert was more of a challenge. Like Piotr, he had a lot of success before we joined forces, but his personality was different and it was harder for him to always accept my advice. Looking back, though, I would say that coaching such two different guys was great experience for me, and when we parted ways I was excited to take on another pupil and continue my new career.

Kristjan Čeh was a young discus phenom from Slovenia who burst onto the scene when he threw 68.75m in June of 2020 when he was only twenty-one years old. Some time before the 2021 Olympics, Kristjan had separated from his coach. He had also started dating the Estonian hammer thrower Anna Maria Orel, and shortly before the Games she asked if I would keep Kristjan company a little bit in Tokyo. I did, and we got along well.

I was impressed by Kristjan's performance at the Games. He finished fifth with a best throw of 66.37m, and I could see he had a lot of potential. Because of his relationship with Anna Maria, he was planning on being in Estonia a lot, so us working together seemed like a logical next step.

It was exciting to take over as the coach of one of the best young discus throwers in the history of the sport, a guy whose size (2.06m tall with a wingspan of approximately

2.15m) and explosiveness made him a potential World and Olympic champion and maybe even a future World Record holder. But it was also intimidating to be entrusted with this precious diamond of an athlete. As I mentioned earlier, Vésteinn always regretted the mistakes he made with Magnús Hallgrímsson, the first athlete he ever trained. Magnús qualified for the Olympic Games in 2000 when he was twenty-four years old, but afterwards never competed in another major championships, and for this Vésteinn blamed himself. But probably not many people noticed when Magnús's career stalled out, because they had never heard of him. But after the 2021 season, everyone who followed the sport knew about Kristjan Čeh, and if his career went badly under my care, it might be the end for me as a coach.

Luckily, I had learned a lot not only from my time training with Vésteinn and Indrek, but also from my three years of coaching Piotr Małachowski and Robert Urbanek. So I believed I was ready to help Kristjan unlock some more of his potential. As it turned out, I was correct.

In 2022, Kristjan had an historic season, including three 70-meter performances at Diamond League meetings and a gold medal at the 2022 World Championships in Eugene where he set a new Championships record with a throw of 71.13m. The record he broke, by the way, was the one Virgilius set to beat me at the 2005 Worlds.

And in a funny coincidence, Virgilius's son Mykolas stepped forward as Kristjan's main rival that summer. Mykolas took the silver in Eugene by throwing 69.27m, and with the top two guys at the 2021 Olympics, Daniel Ståhl and Simon Pettersson, not having their best season it looked like the European Championships might also come down to a battle of Kristjan v. Mykolas.

Kristjan was in top shape after the World Championships. Around that time, he did a 190k power clean, which for someone so tall was very impressive. And in his next competition after Worlds he threw 71.23m in Hungary.

But when we arrived in Munich a few days prior to the European Championships, his back was bothering him. For someone his size, flying is always a challenge, so it was not unusual for his back to feel stiff. We went to a physio for treatment, but unfortunately the physio went too hard with him and made the problem worse. With the competition coming up in a couple of days, this caused us a lot of stress. Luckily, we were able to get Kristjan with a physio we had worked with in Estonia, and he helped relieve some of the stiffness.

He must have done a good job, because Kristjan went out and broke the European Championships record on his first attempt in qualification by throwing 69.06m.

But the back issues caught up with him in the final. It was not so much that he was in pain, but from his first warmup throws on the outfield, it was easy to see he was not himself. Kristjan fouled his first attempt, while a few others opened well. Mykolas threw 66.67, Daniel 66.39m, Simon Pettersson 67.12m, and Lawrence Okoye threw a season's best of 67.14m to take an early lead.

But none of those guys were able to build much on their openers, and Kristjan took over the lead in the second round with a throw of 67.62m. He improved to 67.81m in round three, with Mykolas right behind him at 67.26m.

Then in round five Mykolas hit 69.78m for a new European Championships record. Kristjan came right back with his best throw of the night, 68.28m, but was not able to catch Mykolas.

It was brought up in Estonian media that I never won the Europeans myself, so maybe it was karma that my pupil did not win. But I was proud of Kristjan for coming back with his best throw after Mykolas jumped him. I saw Virgilijus at the airport on the flight back home and congratulated him on how well Mykolas was doing at such a young age. We were able to have a long chat before boarding our flights, and it was great to see him and to relive some of the old days.

All in all, I was quite happy with how my first year with Kristjan went. He had five meets over 70 meters, with three over 71 meters, and he improved his season's average from 66.78m in 2021 to 68.62m in 2022. Based on that, he was excited about defending his title in Budapest in 2023.

Our off-season training went very well, and Kristjan competed at a high level all summer. The difference in 2023 was that Daniel had found his rhythm again. The two of them put on an epic show at the Heino Lipp Memorial meeting in June where Daniel went 71.45m but still lost when Kristjan threw 71.86m. Mykolas had also thrown 71 meters at a meet in the US in April, so it was clear that Kristjan would be in for a fight in Budapest.

Then, one month before the Worlds, he hit a rough patch. After throwing 70.54m at the Slovenian Championships on July 9th, Kristjan stayed at home for a while, but it was quite hot where he lived and he started having trouble sleeping. It would have been best at that point for me to modify his training, but we had a breakdown in our communication and I did not realize he was struggling.

During this period, he lost his feeling at the start of his throw and his distances fell off. He threw 67.60m and finished third at the Gyulai István Memorial in Hungary, then 66.02m for another third place at the Diamond League meeting in London.

He continued to struggle in training when he returned to Estonia, but we kept working and finally at a meet held in the home town of Anna Maria, he found his rhythm again and produced a solid series with a best of 69.99m.

He was consistent again in the Budapest qualification rounds, putting all three throws over 65 meters with a best of 65.95m, and he felt great on the day of the final. We took a couple of standing throws in the outfield, then a couple of non-reverse fulls, and one of them looked to be 69 meters, which would have been a non-reverse PB.

His good feeling continued in the competition. Our strategy in a final was always to open a "safe" throw at less than one hundred percent effort to minimize the risk of fouling. In Budapest, Kristjan's "safe" throw went 68.31m.

Our strategy on the second throw was to add just a little bit to the opener before bombing away in rounds three to six. Kristjan managed this perfectly by throwing 69.27m, which gave him a sizable lead over Mykolas, who was in second with a best of 67.08m. Daniel seemed to be struggling. He opened with 63.01m, then 66.58m, and then a foul. This put him in fourth place behind Kristjan, Mykolas, and Fedrick Dacres, and as each round went by I thought Daniel's chance of challenging for a medal got less and less as it was very hot that night and I did not see how a guy his size could maintain his energy.

Then the fourth round started and Matthew Denny woke everybody up by throwing a PB of 68.24m. Daniel followed with 69.37m to take the lead, and Mykolas jumped back ahead of Denny with a throw of 68.85m.

Kristjan could not respond in rounds four or five, so he was still in second behind Daniel when he stepped in for his final attempt. When we spoke before his throw, I told him to just go for it, and I guess he did because he hit 70.02m to take the lead.

I was screaming in the stands, but I also knew that Daniel had the final throw and could not be counted out, even in hot conditions.

He proved my suspicions correct by unleashing the greatest throw in major championships history, 71.46m! For the first time ever in a championships, 70 meters took second place.

But I was extremely proud of Kristjan. He worked hard to find his feel again after struggling in the weeks before the Worlds, and he produced a 70-meter throw under big pressure on the big stage in Budapest.

Unfortunately, this would be our final season together. As we began preparing for the 2024 season, with the Paris Olympics as the ultimate goal, our ability to communicate broke down to the point where it could not be repaired. Finally, in the spring we decided to part ways.

Over the course of my career, I learned the importance of maintaining cooperation between athlete and coach. Having a healthy cooperation is more important than whatever system of training a coach prefers. Even if, from a scientific point of view, the methodology of training is not the best, it can still work if the athlete and coach work together and believe in what they are doing. Conversely, even the best most scientifically correct system will fail if there is a breakdown in the coach/athlete relationship.

With Kristjan and me unable to get on the same page, it was best for us to go our separate ways. And we parted amicably, with no bitterness.

I have continued to coach the Estonian athlete Gevin Genro Paas, who was a good training partner for Kristjan, and also Moaaz Mohaned Ibrahim from Qatar, who came to me in December of 2022 and in 2023 improved his PB to 63.26m.

As of October of 2024, my coaching career is on hold as I have been elected Vice President of the Estonian Olympic Committee. I am very excited about this position, but who knows? Maybe someday I will get the chance to coach again.

In the meantime, I hope this history of five championship moments in my career will inspire others to make their own dreams come true. With a lot of passion and the right people around you, anything is possible!

With Kristjan Čeh celebrating the gold medal and championships record throw at the 2022 Worlds in Eugene.

Kristjan, Liina, and Gerd at the Farewell Ceremony commemorating Gerd's career.

Gerd was named Estonian Coach of the Year in 2022

Kristjan, Liina, and Gerd.

ABOUT THE AUTHORS

Gerd, Kristjan, and Liina on a family outing.

Photo courtesy of Gerd Kanter

During his career, **Gerd Kanter** won eleven medals at international championships, more than any other male discus thrower. Among those medals were gold at the 2007 World Championships and the 2008 Olympic Games. He was a three-time Athlete of the Year in Estonia, and received the Order of the White Star in recognition of service rendered to his home country. Gerd still holds the unofficial indoor discus World Record of 69.51m. Since retiring in 2018, he has made a successful transition to coaching. Among his pupils have been Piotr Malachowski, Robert Urbanek, Gevin Genro Paas, and Moaaz Mohamed

Ibrahim. Gerd guided the Slovenian Kristjan Čeh to a gold medal and Championships Record at the 2022 World Championships and was subsequently named Coach of the Year in Estonia. He also coached Kristjan Čeh to European and World Championships silver. Gerd lives in Tallinn with his wife Liina and their son Kristjan, He currently works as a Sports Director at Sortsclub Nord and was recently elected as Vice President of the Estonian Olympic Committee. He has teamed with Raul Rebane to publish *Gerd Kanter: 15 Steps to Winning.* Gerd is also the proud uncle of Robin, the son of his sister Ketlin.

Photo courtesy of Alice Wood

At this age, he's just happy to have hair.

Dan McQuaid is a high school throwing coach and retired English teacher who lives with his immensely patient wife in the Chicago suburb of Naperville, Illinois. He has two grown stepsons and a ten-year-old grandson who regularly destroys him in poker and basketball. Dan is proud that his daughter KC has embarked on her own career as a teacher and coach, and plans someday to forgive her for choosing distance running over throwing. He and Roger Einbecker manage the Mcthrows.com website.